Getting started with Sibelius 7

By Darren Jones

Darren Jones
1022 Ringwood Road
West Howe
Bournemouth
Dorset
BH11 9LA
UK

Tel 07971 521403

email: darren@musictechtuition.com
web site: www.musictechtuition.com

First Edition 2013

©2013 Darren Jones

ISBN 978-1-291-46835-9

All rights reserved. No part of this publication may be reproduced or transmitted in any form, including photocopying and recording, without the written permission of the copyright holder, application for which should be addressed to the address above. Such written permission must also be obtained before any part of this publication is stored in an information retrieval system of any nature.

Sibelius is a registered trademarks of Avid Technology, Inc. or its subsidiaries in the United States and/or other countries. All other trademarks are property of their respective copyright holders.

Contents

Sibelius 7 1
Starting Sibelius 1
The Score Window 3
    Moving around the score 3
    Playback 3
Entering Notes 4
    Inputting some music 4
    Editing what you've done 6
    More than one note at a time 6
Selecting a passage 7
      Adding other elements 9
Dynamics and other instructions 12
      Adding articulation 12
Altering barlines 13
Changing Clefs 14
Altering the key 15
Transposing 16
Creating Tuplets 17
Voices 17
Guitar 18
    Chord parts 18
    Tablature 23
    Create an Instrument 23
Drums 25
    Entering drums manually 25
    Bass Drum 26
    Open Hi-Hats 27
Using the ideas panel 28
Spacing and Layout 30
Creating a score and parts from scratch 31
Repeating a section 34
Finishing touches 39
The Mixer 40
    Mixer channel types 41
Creating Parts 42
Plug-Ins 43
    Brass Fingerings 43

    Adding Harmony 43

        Note Names 44

Transformations 44

    Double.. 44

    Halve 44

    Retrograde 45

    Invert.. 45

    Augment Intervals... 45

    Diminish Intervals.. 45

    Randomize Pitches 46

    Rotate Pitches 46

Arranging... 47

    Creating your source material.. 47

    Creating the Arrangement 48

    Arranging into a new Score 51

    Summary 55

Score Styles 55

Exporting your work... 56

    PDF 56

    MIDI.. 56

    Audio 56

Keyboard Shortcuts 57

    File related 57

    Creating Notes.. 57

    Adding elements 57

The Star Spangled Banner 58

Introduction

This book is intended to give you a solid grounding in the use of Sibelius 7 for creating scores and sequenced music. It will take the complete beginner on a tour of the features of the software that are most likely to be used by the everyday student or user of it, and then go through the preparation of a score of a piece of music, as well as look at arrangement of a piece using Sibelius' arrange function.

While it is aimed squarely at those who have never used the software before, the changes in interface made for Sibelius 7 will also help anyone making the transition from the original menu-based look if Sibelius from version 6 and before to Sibelius 7's new 'ribbon' interface.

The book follows closely the notes made during workshops teaching Sibelius to classes of GCSE and A-level students who are using the software for the first time, and as a result should be useful for anyone taking a music course where Sibelius skills are needed.

Conventions used in this book

In an attempt to make the text of the book clearer, some formatting has been used throughout. Whenever there is a button or text on screen which you need to read, alter or click, it has been **presented in this font**.

Whenever there is a keyboard shortcut given, it has been **presented in this font**. All the keyboard shortcuts given are the defaults; while there are many which could be edited to make working within Sibelius easier, referring to custom keyboard shortcuts would make matters less clear. Remember that keyboard shortcuts will make working in Sibelius much quicker and easier, so some of the most useful ones have been included on page 57.

Getting started with Sibelius 7

By Darren Jones

Sibelius 7

Unlike other music software, Sibelius is primarily for the production of scores and parts in traditional notation. It is possible to use Sibelius to play back the music via a MIDI synthesizer, but it is not a traditional 'sequencer' in the sense that Cubase and Logic are. However, being aimed at the score-creation market it offers a far greater range of tools than those offered by combined sequencers.

Starting Sibelius

When you first start Sibelius you will see a splash screen like the one below:

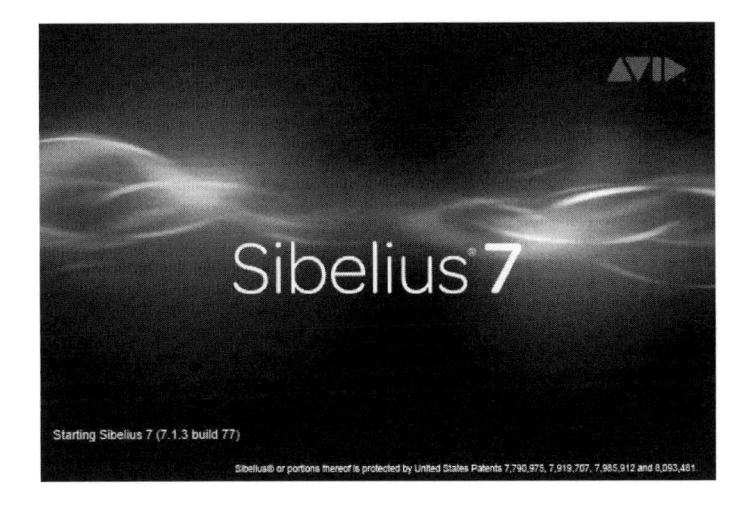

Once it has finished loading (which can take a while) you will see the Quick Start screen, as seen below.

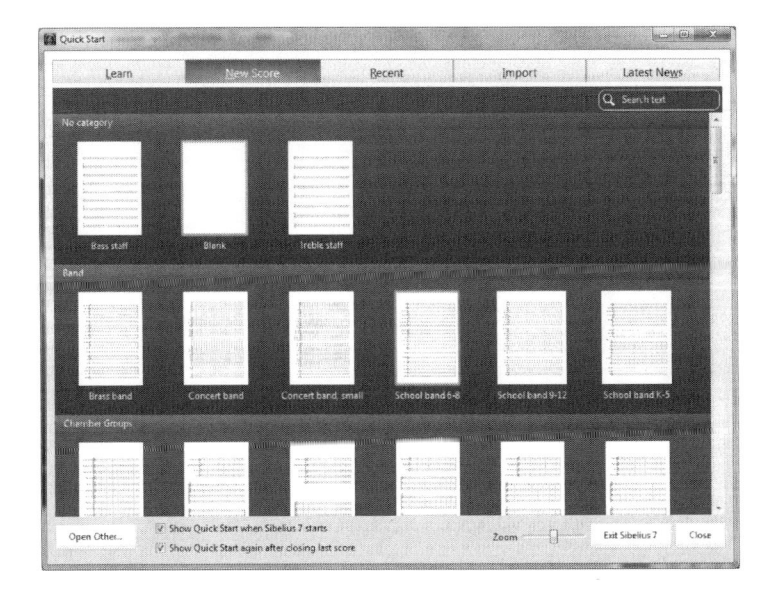

Here there are a number of templates to choose from, but we will start with a blank score to allow us to create exactly what we want. Click the Blank template (second one on the top row), and you will go to the next screen.

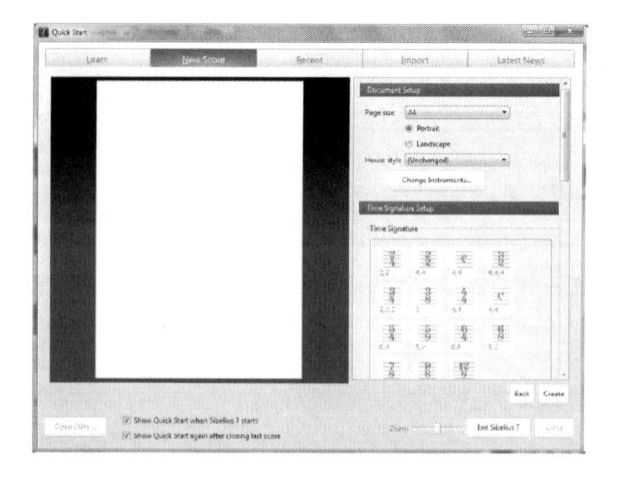

Here we need to choose the options for the score, and as the score is blank we need to add some instruments to create music on. To do that, click `Change Instruments` on the right-hand side of the window, and you'll see another window:

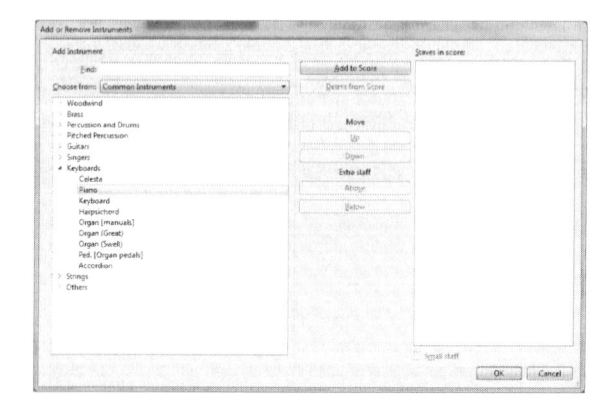

Here any of Sibelius' many instruments can be added, and in this case we want a plain treble staff, which is found under `Others` on the left-hand side of the window. Once you have selected it, click `Add to score` and it will appear in the right-hand column, as seen next:

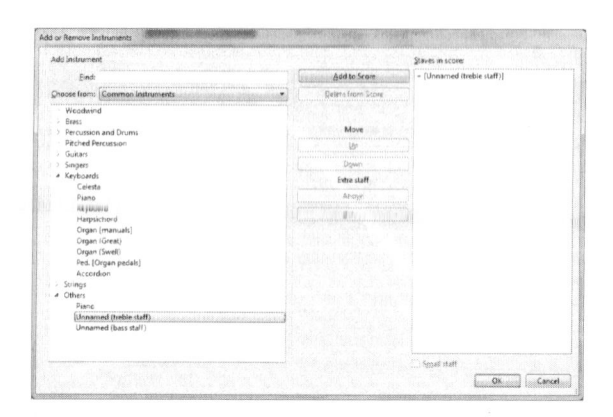

The Score Window

Once you have created your instrument(s), click OK and you will see the main Sibelius window, as below:

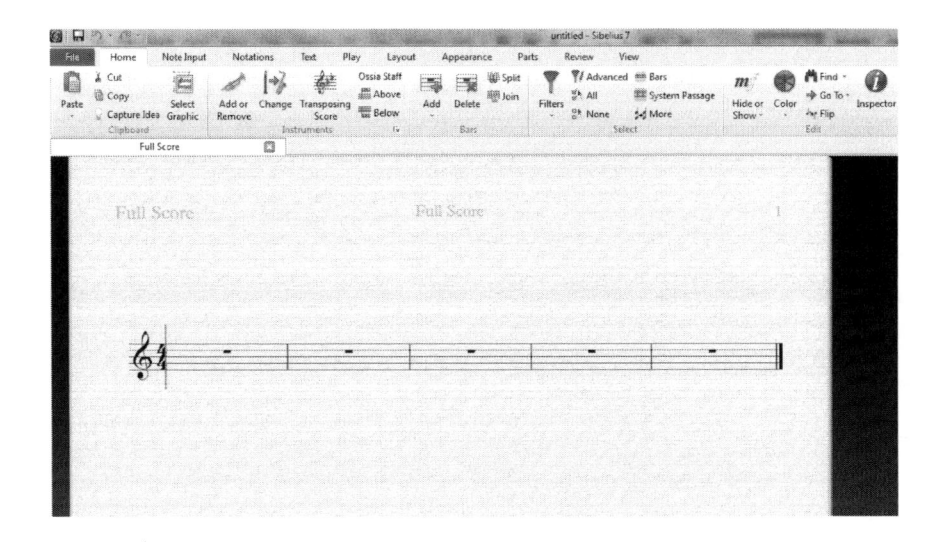

The score takes up the majority of the page, with a ribbon-type toolbar across the top (much like Word 2007) with most of the features you need available there. There are a great many of them, but we will cover the most commonly used items, and how to navigate around the score.

Moving around the score

Sibelius has a few ways of moving around the score - you can either use the scrollbars, or you can click-and-drag on the 'paper' of your score to move it. Note that you need to do this on a blank section of the page, and as you move it the cursor will turn into a hand.

There is a zoom control at the bottom right; this defaults to 100%, but it's possible to zoom in or out using this, to view an entire page or zoom right in to make some detailed changes - just select the appropriate scale from the menu.

At first when using Sibelius there are several actions that seem counter-intuitive particularly after using other scoring packages (or word processing programs), but spending some time using Sibelius will pay off. Note that you cannot marquee (click and drag) around items with a box as you can with many other programs - we will see later on how you select more than one item.

Playback

You can play your piece at any time - **SPACE** will start and stop the playback. **P** will play the score from wherever you have a note selected. **CTRL+[** will move the play position back to the beginning of the score. If you want a transport panel to control playback, go to View > Panels > Transport and you will have complete control of playback and position in the score.

Entering Notes

The next step is to enter some notes. Sibelius offers a number of ways to do this, either via a MIDI keyboard connected to the computer (whether in real or step time), or via the PC's alphanumeric keyboard. To make the most of Sibelius it's best to learn the keyboard shortcuts that it offers, as it can then become as quick and efficient as entering words into a word processor (something that the makers liken it to). There are two elements to entering notes – their pitch and duration. To enter the duration, you use the computer's numeric keypad, which is shown on-screen and to the right.

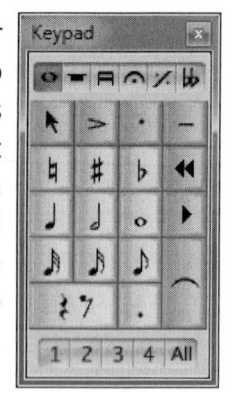

This keypad allows you to quickly change the lengths of the notes or rests you are entering - here, a **4** will enter a crotchet, a **5** will enter a minim and so on. Pressing the **0** key will toggle between entering rests and notes, while keys **1-6** will change the duration, **7-9** will control the pitch (natural/sharp/flat), and so on. This is while the keypad is in the "Common Notes" mode, which it defaults to, and which can be accessed by pressing **F7**. The other modes can be accessed either by clicking on the appropriate small button at the top (under Keypad) where the more notes (**F8**), beams (**F9**), articulations (**F10**), jazz articulations (**F11**) and accidentals (**F12**) buttons are or by pressing the F-key associated with that icon.

The most common use of this keypad is to set note lengths, so we'll stick with it in this default mode.

Note pitches can be entered from a MIDI keyboard, or from the computer's keyboard; this is done using the keys **A** to **G**. The final thing we need to look at before entering some music is to know that the cursor has two main modes. There is the "editing" mode, which uses the normal cursor (white arrow, pointing to the left), but there is also the "notes" mode, which uses a coloured cursor. The easy way to change between modes is to hit the **N** key, which toggles between them.

Inputting some music

We'll input some music to get started; to do this, firstly make sure that you are in the "editing" mode (white cursor).

Once you are, single-click inside the first bar; it should be selected, as seen to the right. You have now told Sibelius where you want to enter your first note (at Bar 1, beat 1).

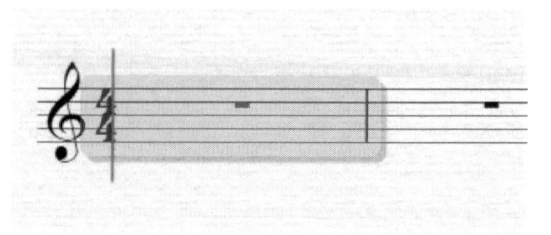

Next, on the numeric keypad, hit 4. This tells Sibelius that you want to insert a crotchet, and it splits the rest up to reflect this.

Now, enter the first note by pressing a **C** on the computer or MIDI keyboard. It should look like the staff on the right. Adding another note...

... will carry the process on (in this case, a D).

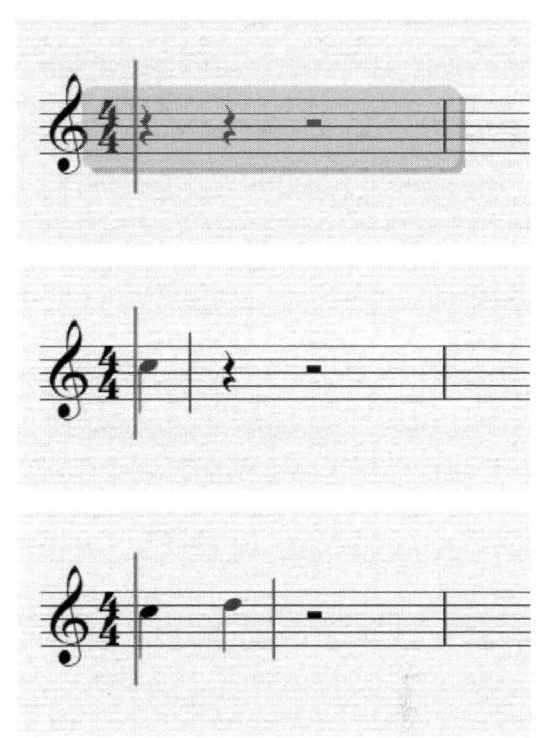

Now let's enter the series of notes that we want. We'll keep things simple and just enter a fragment of a scale, so press (on the PC keyboard) C, D, E, F, G, F, E, D, C.

You should end up with this:

That's a simple example, but it's easy to build up a range of single-note music using these tools with the addition of the knowledge that pressing the space bar creates a rest of the chosen length at the current position. Spend some time working with these tools, entering music, and you'll see that Sibelius always enters the next note at the octave that's closest to the note previous. This can create a problem sometimes, and the way to correct this is to press the note that you want, and then move it to the correct octave by holding down the **CTRL** key and pressing the up or down cursor key; doing so moves the notes by an octave. Note that if you enter the notes via a MIDI keyboard then their pitch is not affected by this, so many people find this more convenient if such a keyboard is available.

Editing what you've done

So far we've seen that it's possible to enter single-note parts quickly and easily using just the PC keyboard to enter the notes, controlling the duration with the keys on the numeric keypad. But what if you want to change what you've done?

The first thing to remember is to change from "notes" mode (coloured cursor) to "edit" mode (white cursor), by pressing **N** Once this is done, it's possible to edit what you've already done. You can either select notes directly (by clicking on the note-heads), or by using the left and right cursor keys to move backwards and forwards through the part. Once you are at the appropriate note, you can do a number of things to it; you can delete it (by pressing **Backspace**), you can change its pitch (diatonically) by pressing the up or down cursor keys, you can alter its octave by holding down **CTRL** and pressing the up or down cursor keys, or you can add (or remove) an accidental from it by pressing **7**, **8** or **9** on the numeric keypad.

More than one note at a time

So far we have only seen how to make monophonic lines, but it's common to want to play intervals and chords. Sibelius makes this easy to do, whether initially inputting a line or editing a previous one, the concept is the same. Simply select a note (or input it), and then press the number key (on the main PC keyboard, not the numeric keypad) that corresponds to the interval that you require. Let's take an example - here is a simple one-octave C major scale, which was inputted using the PC keyboard.

However, to add intervals a third above the notes already present, it's simply a case of selecting the first note (so it is highlighted in blue), and then pressing the **3** key; a note a third above the first C (E) is created, as seen below.

It's then a case of moving to the next note (using the right cursor key is quickest), and then repeating the process to end up with the scale as shown on the next page.

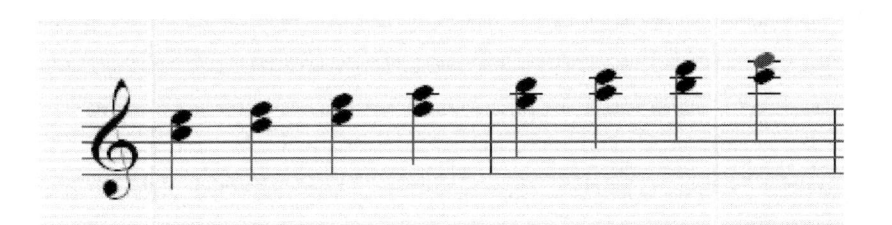

If the scale was required to be harmonised in seventh chords, it would just be a case of pressing **3** three times on each note before moving on; each time a new note a diatonic third will be created above the current one. In this way it's quick and easy to build up harmony.

This harmony does not have to be added after the initial input of the notes; it's possible to do it as the original entering is taking place, pressing the appropriate keys before moving on to the next note.

Selecting a passage

The tools you already have are sufficient to create quite a range of music, but there is clearly a lot more to learn.

Selecting notes we have already seen, whether clicking individual note-heads or using the cursor keys; however, it's often useful to be able to select entire bars, staves or entire parts, as well as groups of notes or phrases.

We have already seen how to select an entire bar; to recap, just click somewhere inside the bar (but not on a note); the whole bar and all its contents are highlighted.

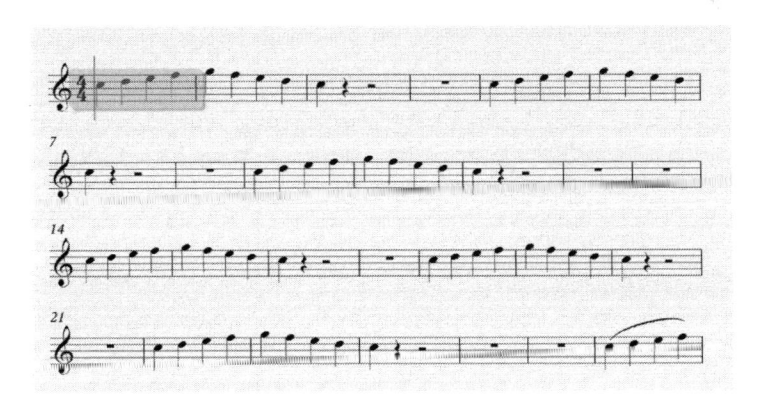

To select all the bars on one line, double-click in the same place; all the bars of the current instrument are selected.

To select the instrument throughout the current score, triple-click in the same way.

Note the zig-zag ends of each line that is selected, showing that the selection carries on (in this case off the screen onto another page).

If you want to select a different number of bars, select the first bar as shown above, and then hold down **SHIFT** while selecting the final bar that you want; all the bars between will be selected too.

If you want to select other amounts of music (such as a couple of beats), click on one of the notes at the first position that you want, and then hold down **SHIFT** and click on a note at the last beat that you want. The blue highlight will show that you've highlighted the beats between the two.

If you want to select a single beat (chord or interval), then click a note in that beat, and hold down **SHIFT** and press the up cursor (↑). The box will highlight only the beat you selected.

It is quite common to need to repeat passages, either to be repeated or to act as the basis for a variation. Sibelius makes this simple; just select the note, chord, phrase or passage that you want to repeat (using the techniques outlined above), and press the **R** key.

Adding other elements

Although notes are an important part of any musical score, there is a great deal of information that is not note-based, things such as dynamic markings, key and time signatures, note symbols and so on. Being capable of such a wide range of scoring, Sibelius provides a wide variety of such symbols. One way to add these is to right-click on the manuscript paper, and a menu appears, as shown on the right. There are a wide range of elements that we can add, so we'll look at the most common items, but the procedure to add any of these items is the same;

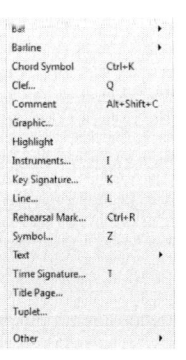

9

right-click to get the menu to appear, and then select the item that you want (in the case of some of these items there are sub-menus which appear). Once you have selected this then the cursor will change to "Insert" mode (in colour) – now to place the item, left-click in the appropriate location.

As with so many actions in Sibelius, the common elements have keyboard shortcuts for them; knowing these will aid your speed at creating scores. Let's now look at some of these items.

One of the most common markings to add is a slur or phrase mark; Sibelius treats these as the same thing. The quickest way to enter one of these is to select the notes that you want to be covered by the mark (or just the one if you want a slur), and then press the **S** key. An example is shown below.

This shows the original two-bar phrase.

Select the first note (either with the cursor keys or mouse), and press **S** to get a slur.

Selecting the entire first bar (clicking in space within the bar), and pressing **S** generates a phrase mark.

Once the slur has been created, it's possible to move it around; you'll notice that if you select an end of the slur with the mouse it turns blue, and square "handles" appear, which can be used to alter the slur's position, shape and size. The handles at the ends allow the length and position to be altered, while the middle bottom one allows movement of the entire slur. The handles at the top control the shape.

Any such item such as lines, slurs, etc, is attached to a note. This is not always immediately apparent, but if you move the start handle away from the note (as shown on the left), you'll see a dotted grey line which shows which note the item is attached to. This is an important concept, as if any items are attached to the wrong notes (or the wrong staves), then when creating parts from a score (which we will look at later on), the markings would end up on the wrong parts.

Dynamic markings (crescendos and diminuendos) can be applied in a similar manner, and the shortcut to create them is **H** (they were previously called 'hairpins'). Select a note and hit the **H** key, and one will appear under the staff. If you want a diminuendo, hold **SHIFT+H**, in the same way. As with the slurs, selecting a passage of music before creating the mark will make it the length selected, saving time. In the same way as all such markings, they have 'handles' that allow their movement, so if the hairpin is not the correct size, you can resize it as you wish. The phrase below had these markings added by selecting the first bar and pressing **H**, and then the second bar and **SHIFT+H**

The Ribbon
All of the elements we have seen so far are also available on the ribbon menu at the top of the screen. To access them, click Notations and you will see it as below:

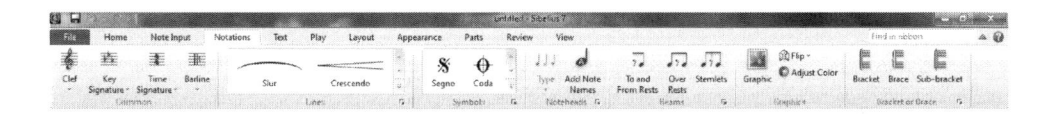

Here it's possible to visually select the slur or crescendo, and clicking the 'More' button as seen to the right will display the full range of available lines that can be added.

As can be seen, there are a wide range of lines available, but it's a good idea to learn the keyboard shortcuts for the most common ones - if you get in the habit of using them, you will work much faster than solely with the mouse.

Dynamics and other instructions

To add dynamic markings such as *mp*, *f*, etc, select a note and hit **CTRL+E** (for expression) - you will see that a flashing cursor appears, and you can now enter the dynamic markings you want. To get authentic-looking letters, hold down **CTRL** while typing the appropriate letters. Click elsewhere when finished. Note that Sibelius will use these dynamic instructions for playback.

The instructions that you can add are not limited to the dynamics mentioned above - common instructions to add are available from a word menu which appears if you right-click while entering expression text. It is shown below:

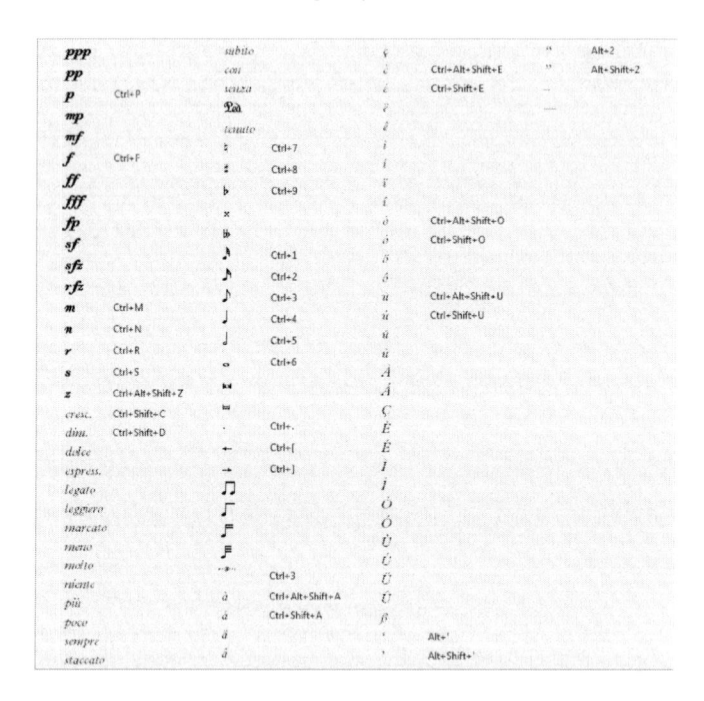

Any item from it can be selected with the mouse, or by using the keyboard shortcuts which are shown next to each one. Note that the menu doesn't have to be visible to use these, so you can memorise common entries – the **CTRL+F** and **CTRL+P** shortcuts we have already seen are there, amongst others.

Adding articulation

Often parts need to have articulation marks added to them. These marks are added to each note (being attached to them), and this is done by changing the mode of the numeric keypad. You may recall that it defaults to changing the note length, but can perform other actions. Press **F11**, and the keypad window will change to look like the one to the right. This shows that they keypad will now enter various articulation marks. If you are unsure of what any of these marks mean, hover the mouse pointer above the appropriate key, and the meaning will pop up. In this case we want to add some bowing marks, which are also commonly used to indicate plectrum strokes with guitar parts. The first note is selected, and then the appropriate keypad button is pressed (in this case, **6** to generate a 'downbow' mark). The next note is then selected (using the cursor → key), and then **5** pressed to create an 'upbow' mark. This is followed throughout the phrase to show that alternate picking is required throughout, generating the phrase shown below.

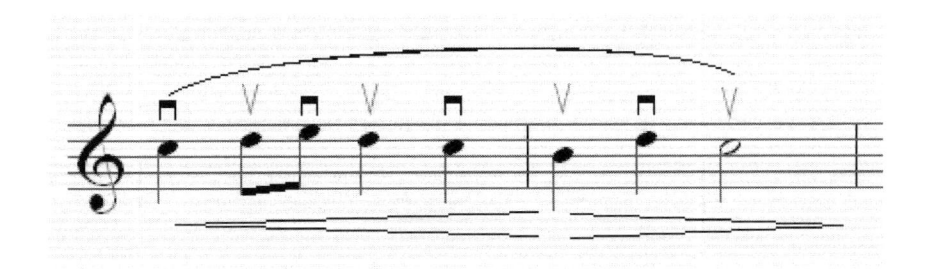

Any other articulation marks can be added using the same techniques, and these marks can all be moved, but unlike others we have looked at, they cannot be moved horizontally, only vertically, as clearly they need to be above the appropriate note.

Altering barlines

By default, Sibelius uses standard single barlines, with a thick double barline to denote the last bar of the piece. However, other barlines are often wanted, such as double barlines to denote section changes, etc. These can easily be added by right-clicking and selecting the `Barline` menu; a new menu pop-out appears (shown right), and the appropriate barline can be chosen; the cursor now becomes the coloured 'insert' cursor, and clicking on the appropriate barline will change it to the desired type. Note that these options are all available from the Barline menu on the notations ribbon, with their appearances shown as well.

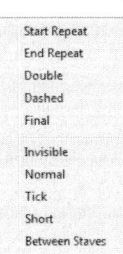

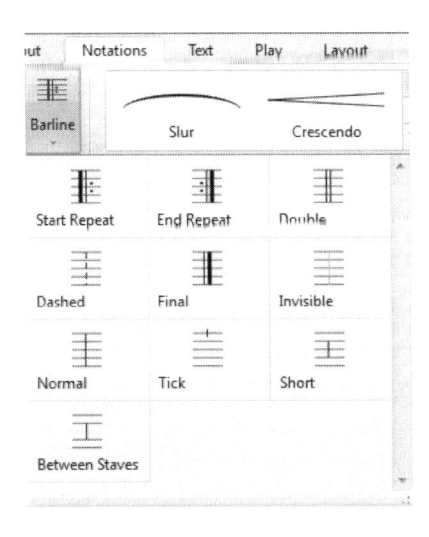

13

It's also possible to select the barline you want to alter *before* using either of these methods, and then the one you have selected will be altered as soon as you choose the type of barline you want. As with dynamic instructions, if you have entered start and end repeat bars, Sibelius will obey them on playback.

Changing Clefs

In much the same way, selecting the 'clef' option (or hitting **Q**) brings up the clef dialog; choose the clef that you want and then click on the staff where you want the clef change to occur.

As with much use of Sibelius, selecting an appropriate passage before summoning the menu can save a lot of time. If you have a short passage which needs a new clef before returning to the original, select the passage first:

Selecting the bass clef now leads only the selected passage to have that clef applied.

Altering the key

By default, Sibelius will create the staff in the key of C Major. To change the composition's key (whether initially, or at any point in the piece), right-click and select `Key Signature` (or press **K**), and the key signature menu will appear:

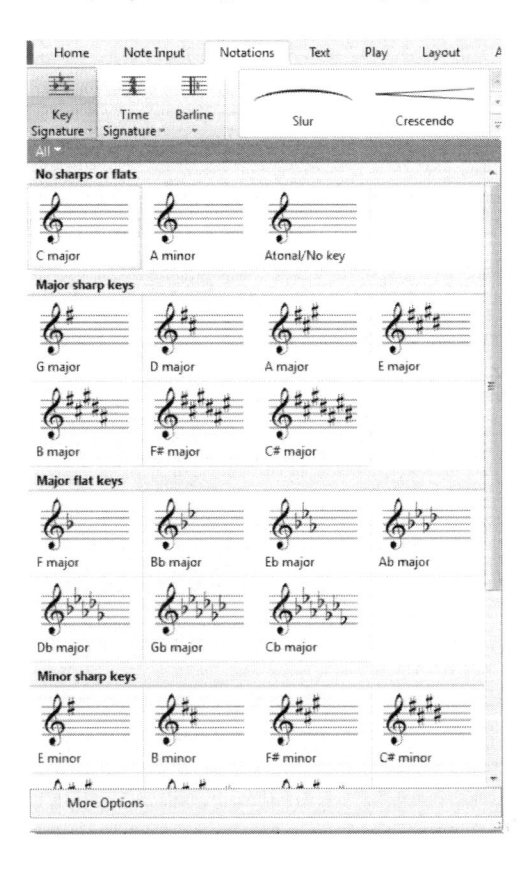

Now, choose the key that you want, and click where you want the key change to occur - again, as with the clef selection, note that you can select a passage and the key change will only be applied to that passage.

Note that now entering any notes via the PC keyboard will lead them to be in that key, so entering an F while in G major will create an F♯. Also, remember that inserting the keychange after the music has been created will mean Sibelius inserts any accidentals that are needed to keep the pitches as they were when originally entered - the passage below is an extreme example to illustrate this:

Transposing

Sometimes you will want to alter the key of a passage that you have already entered - for a new section, or to change the key for a particular instrument or performer. Sibelius will do this for you, saving much work in transposition. First, select the passage that you want to transpose:

Then go to the transpose dialogue, which can be found by hitting **SHIFT+T** or going to the `Note Input` section of the ribbon, and clicking `Transpose`:

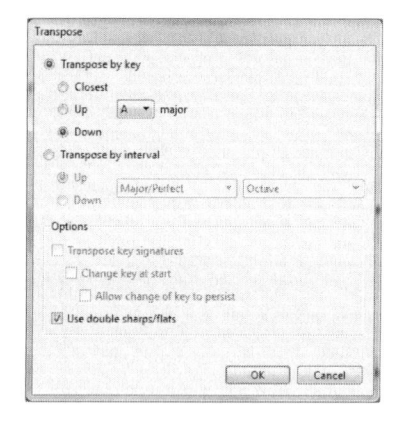

Here the options have been set for the required transposition - you can pick whether to take the passage up or down, or to the closest, and then the key that you want it transposed to - in this case taking the passage from the original key of C Major (which Sibelius takes from the score) and transposing it into A Major.

Changing the key signature will complete the transposition if required.

Creating Tuplets

Often tuplets are used in music (triplets are the most common), and creating them in Sibelius involves a couple of steps. The steps are outlined below, in this case for a triplet:

Firstly, create a note of the appropriate value for the triplet. In this case we want some quarter-note triplets, so we'll create a quarter-note.

Secondly, press (**CTRL+3**), and the triplets will be created, with rests for the second and third notes.

Now entering the second note creates it as we would expect

Finally, entering the third note completes the triplet.

Sibelius can create anything from duplets (press **CTRL+2**) to nontuplets (**CTRL+9**); the correct initial note value needs to be selected, and if it wouldn't fit in the space available, then Sibelius will let you know that it would be too long.

Voices

It is a common requirement to use separate voices when writing a piece of music, whether to notate vocal harmonies, or separate an orchestral section into smaller divisions. You may have noticed that Sibelius by default uses blue to highlight the notes and cursor. This is because blue is the colour for voice 1, the default voice. However, Sibelius can use up to four voices, and the voice that you are currently working with can be changed by holding down **ALT** and pressing **1** to **4** on the main PC keyboard. You will notice that the colour of any highlighted buttons on the graphic keypad will change, from blue (voice 1), to green (voice 2), yellow (voice 3) and pink (voice 4). The colours only show when the notes are highlighted, but this gives the flexibility to notate separate lines and voices on the same staff. To change a note (or group of notes) to another voice, simply select it/them, and right-click; the menu will have a "voice" option, and you can pick the voice you wish them to be. You can also (of course) do this from the keyboard, by holding **ALT** and pressing the number key of the voice you want to set them as.

Guitar

There are a number of options available for notation for the guitar - some guitarists read standard notation, but many do not, and in some cases it is preferable to provide just chords and a rhythm to leave the part open to interpretation. We will now look at a couple of options for guitar notation.

Chord parts

For a chord part, we'll not use 'traditional' notation, but instead create a guitar chord part, with the rhythm written on a single-note staff, and add chord symbols above - something that many guitarists find much easier to read.

To do this, we will need to edit the Instruments available to us (to create the an instrument which only uses a single-line staff to show the rhythm, but is still called a guitar). You will only need to do this once - Sibelius will remember it for future use.

First, go to the `Home` tab, and click the arrow at the bottom right of the `Instruments` section. You will see the Edit Instruments dialogue box, as below.

We want to create a guitar instrument based on an existing guitar, so in the left-hand pane click on `Common Instruments`. In the next pane (`Families in Ensemble`), click `Guitars`. In the next pane, the guitars will be listed.

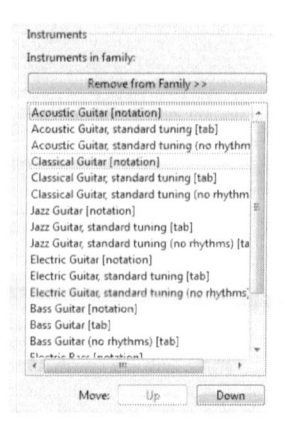

Click on `Acoustic Guitar [notation]` and click `New Instrument....` you'll see the following dialogue box, asking if you're sure you want to create it.

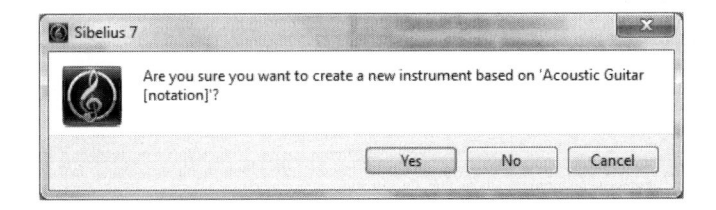

Click `Yes`, and you will see a screen like the following one:

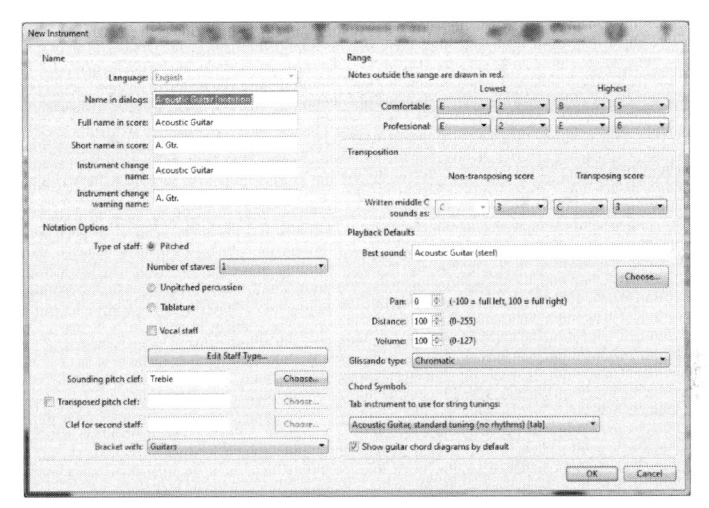

This window allows you to alter the properties of guitar instruments, including the names (seen at top right), the staff, and also which sounds are played. There are two areas to change - firstly the name that will appear, and to change the staff to be a single line to show only the rhythm.

First, change the names - set them as below:

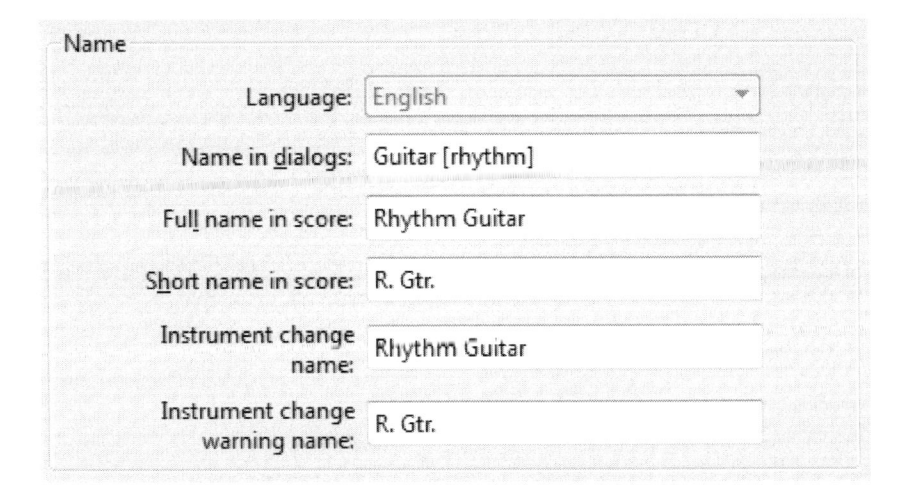

Next, the staff needs to be changed to a single-note one. This is done by clicking `Edit Staff Type...` which will lead to the next dialogue box:

Under `Staff`, change the `Number of Staff Lines` to 1. Click `OK` to close the Staff Type box, and click `OK` to close the instrument edit box.

You have now created a single-line guitar to use. Close the Edit Instruments box, and now go to add a new Instrument (I). The guitar will not be in the Common Instruments group, so click on the `Choose From` menu and pick `All Instruments`. Expanding the Acoustic Guitar group will now list the `Guitar [rhythm]` instrument you just created, so add it to the score.

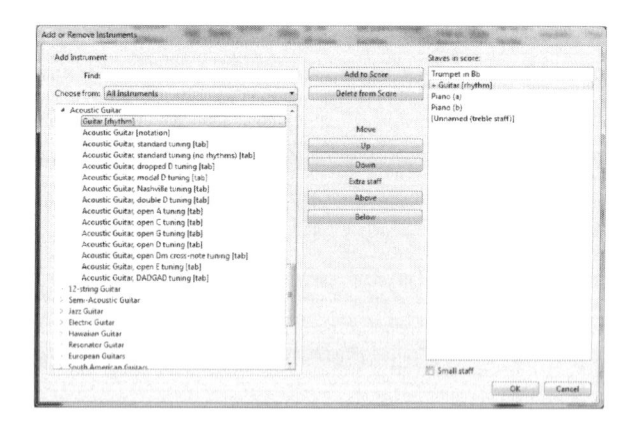

Here is the score with the blank guitar part:

As you can see, the staff is now a typical single-note staff, and now it's a case of adding the notes in in the same way as with other parts. On this particular staff, B is the central note, so we'll enter the rhythm of the guitar part as that note. Once it's been added, it should look like the part shown below. Note that it will not play back correctly, but we aren't too worried about this as creating effective-sounding guitar parts is quite involving, and beyond the scope of this tutorial.

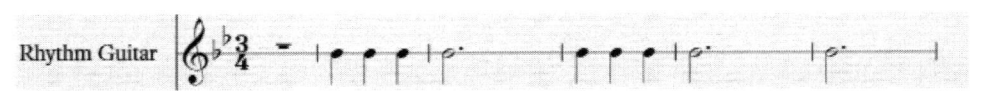

The next stage is to change the note heads; guitar parts typically use note-heads that look like slashes, so we'll do the same here. To do this, we need to explore a new part of the Notations tab of the ribbon. Click Notations and then click the Type button under note heads:

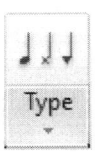

The menu showing the note head types available will then appear:

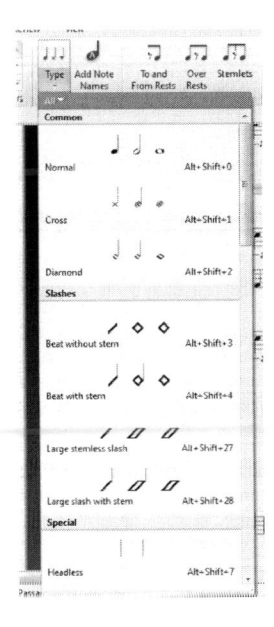

The desired note heads can be chosen from this menu - Beat with stem was chosen, leading the guitar to look like this:

21

Now we can see that this is looking much more like a guitar part. But we need to tell the player what to play, by adding chord symbols. These are found on the Text tab of the ribbon, so click Text and you should see the relevant area:

Clicking `Chord Symbol` will turn the cursor to insertion mode (unless you've already selected a note, when you will be entering a chord for it), and clicking a note will allow you to enter the name of the chord using the keyboard. In this case, an E♭ was entered by pressing **EB** on the keyboard. If you hit **TAB** or click away with the mouse, the text will be transformed into the correct notation, and a chord symbol will be provided by Sibelius for the chord in question:

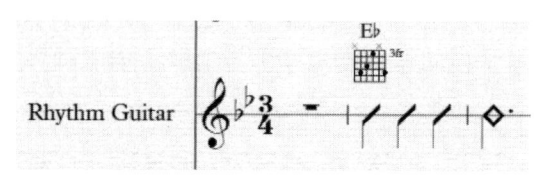

Sibelius will pick the chord from its bank of chord symbols. If the one shown is the wrong one, you can get Sibelius to show alternatives by clicking the revoice chord diagram button, shown below:

Sibelius will then show you an alternative, and clicking the button again will cycle through the other options - here are the options for E♭.

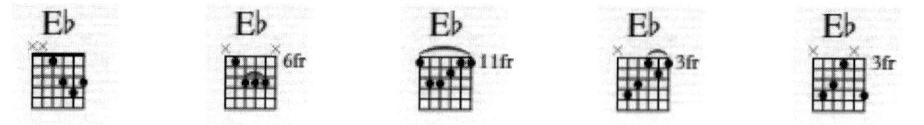

You can add chords quickly to the piece by this method, and if you hit **TAB** when you've entered the chord, Sibelius will move on to the next note, ready for you to enter a chord there (to skip to the next note, press **TAB** again).

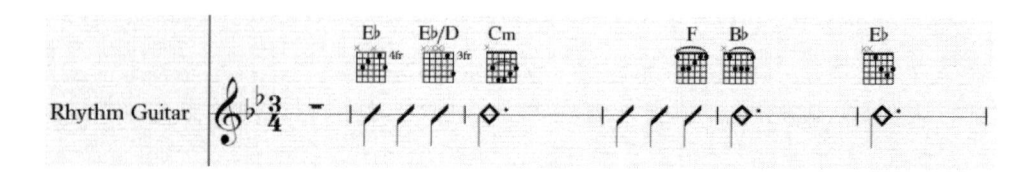

Tablature

Tablature (TAB) can be a useful notation for guitarists - not only because many don't read standard notation, but also because TAB shows where to play a given note on the guitar - for many there are different options, and if you are a guitarist or know how to play a particular melody it can be useful to convey this information to a reader. If you play the guitar and have been writing music in Sibelius but are not a good reader, converting your part to TAB can help you translate it to the guitar. We will now look at how to create TAB from an existing melody.

Create an Instrument

The first step is to create an instrument for the Tablature, by pressing **I** and from the dialogue box picking an appropriate instrument from the Guitars group - the TAB instruments have `[tab]` written after them. Here `Electric Guitar, standard tuning [tab]` was chosen.

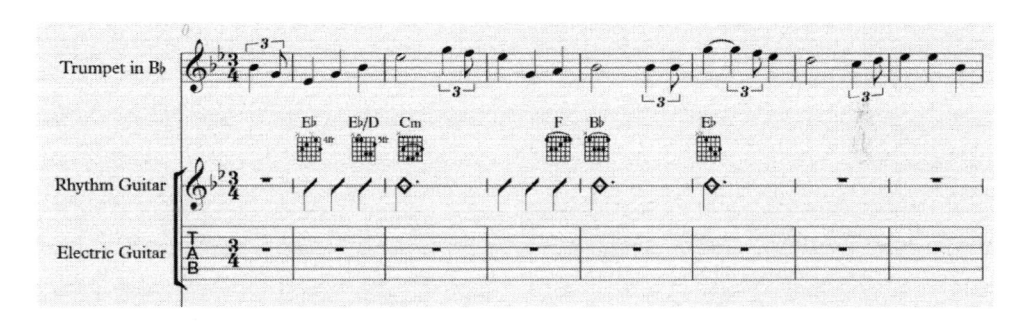

Next, copy the part you want from another staff and paste it onto the guitar tab instrument.

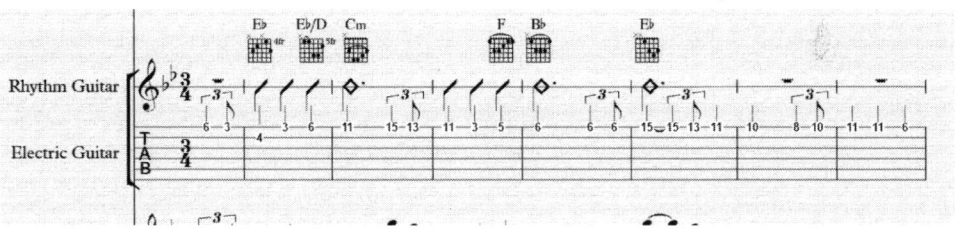

You may find that the staff is too close to that above or below, in which case, click and drag to move it.

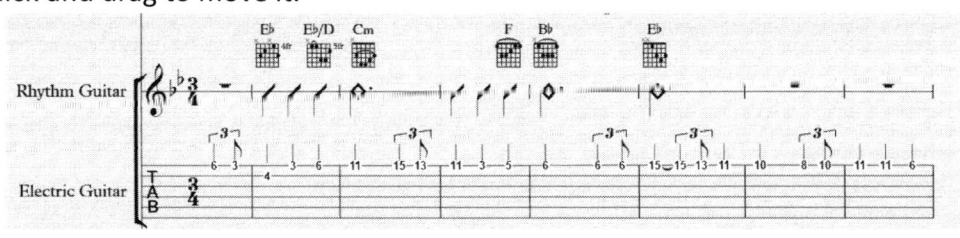

It is not uncommon to find that a melody or part is in the wrong octave range for the guitar - the melody here is all on the top string of the guitar, and is too high. To transpose, select the part you want to transpose and go to the Transpose dialogue box (Note Input > Transpose or **SHIFT+T**) - in this case shifting down by an octave:

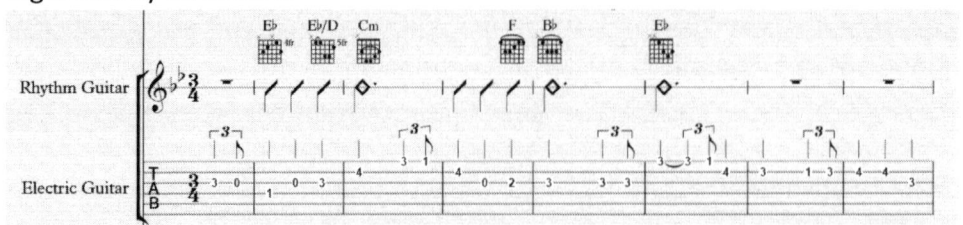

You can see that the melody is now being played across a number of strings, and at a much more suitable range for this arrangement.

Sometimes you may have individual notes that you want to play on a different string. To do this, click and drag the note to the string you want to it be on:

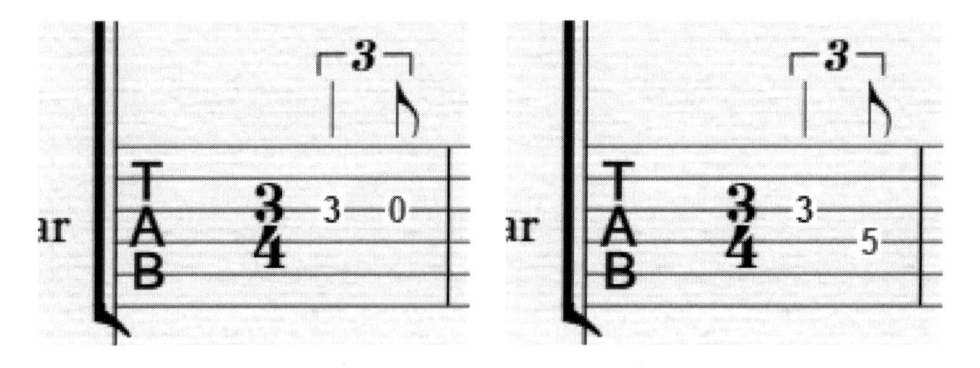

Drums

Drums are a special case - both in terms of notation and what's actually being played - so we'll look at two ways of creating them.

Entering drums manually

The first way we will look at is to create a drum staff and then enter the notes manually. Go to `Home > Instruments > Add or Remove` and create a `Drum Set (Rock)` from the Percussion and Drums group. You will see a staff like this one:

Next, enter some hi hats. These can be done by using your MIDI keyboard, or by using the computer keyboard and pressing **G** - they should be entered above the top line of the staff, as seen in the three steps here.

Note that they will not play in their present state. We need to change the note heads so that they display correctly, and will be played as hi hats. To do this, select the hi hat notes you have entered...

...and go to `Notations > Note Heads > Type`, and from the drop-down menu, pick Cross. You can also do this using **ALT+SHIFT+1**. The note heads will change to crosses, and they will now play as hi hats.

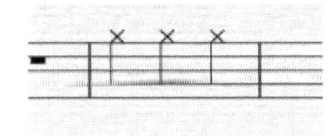

If you enter a minim, then it will have a cross with a circle around it, as seen in the next bar here:

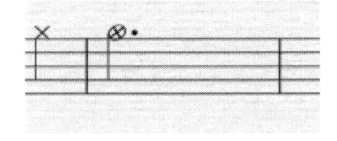

To enter a snare to coincide with a hi-hat, pick the hi-hat in question (here the dotted minim was chosen), and press **SHIFT+5** on the keyboard. The note will appear a fifth below:

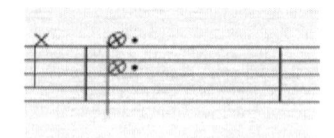

The final step here is to turn it back into a normal note head so it sounds correctly (the cross notation would signify a side stick/rimshot which isn't what we want at the moment, but may be something you want in the future). Again, this can be done from Notations > Note Heads > Type, or you can press **ALT+SHIFT+0**.

Bass Drum

Next we will add the bass drum. In drum notation, this should be notated somewhat separately from the notes we have entered so far, with the bass drum being down-stemmed and the other notes up-stemmed. Once we add the bass drum in, the other notes will be up-stemmed and look correct, but at the moment it will looks something like this:

We will now enter the bass drum. Firstly, change to voice 2 - this is done by clicking in the appropriate place in the keypad window, as seen below. The bass drum will be notated in voice 2, and this will lead to the stems being set correctly.

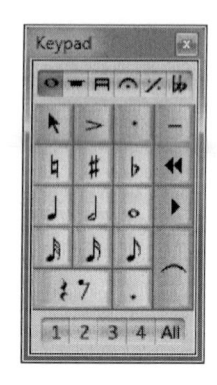

Now, enter the bass drum as you have other parts previously, by entering an F that will appear at the bottom of the clef:

Note that the previous parts are now up-stemmed in this bar, and that the note is highlighted in green. Adding another note is much the same:

Note that each bar may not become up-stemmed in voice 1 until there is a voice 2 note present - observe the difference between bar 2 above and below.

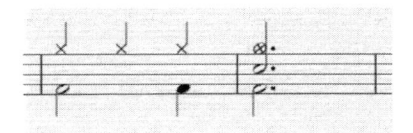

Open Hi-Hats

Hi hats are not always played closed, sometimes they are open, and we can add the notation for this. Select the note you wish to make into an open hi-hat:

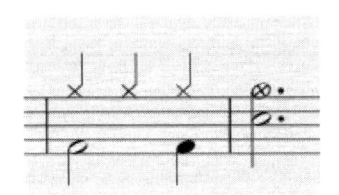

Then change the keypad into Articulations mode (**F10**):

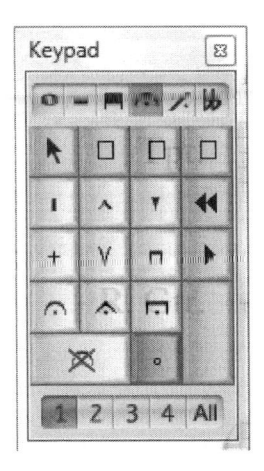

Hit the **.** key on the keypad, and the note will have the open articulation added.

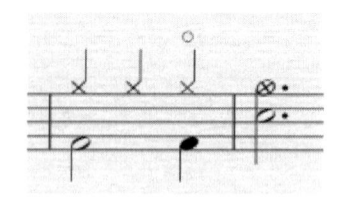

Duplicating the drum part is simply a case of highlighting the bars you want to be repeated:

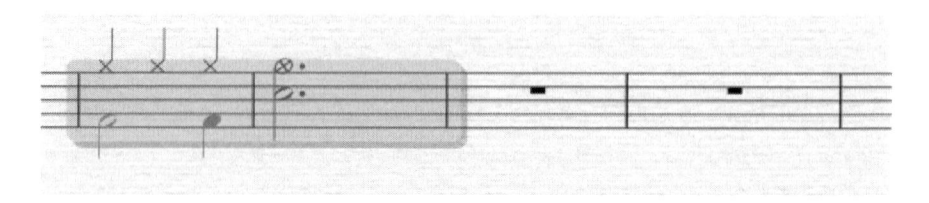

and hitting **R** on the keyboard.

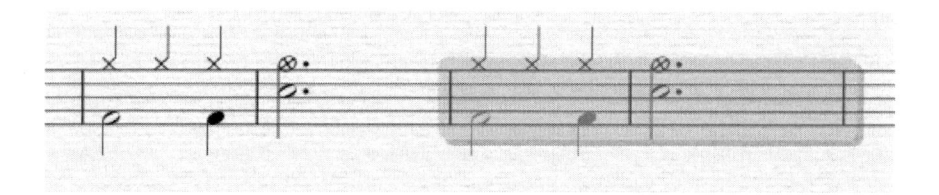

Using the ideas panel

The ideas panel can be useful in a wide range of situations - it provides a library of musical ideas that you can quickly copy and paste into your piece, and then modify to suit your taste where appropriate. It's not just useful for drums, it has a huge range of ideas for you to explore, but we'll look at it for drums as it's often useful for anyone who's not sure what a drum kit should be doing.

Firstly, make sure the ideas panel is visible. This is done from `View > Panels` and selecting `Ideas` as seen below.

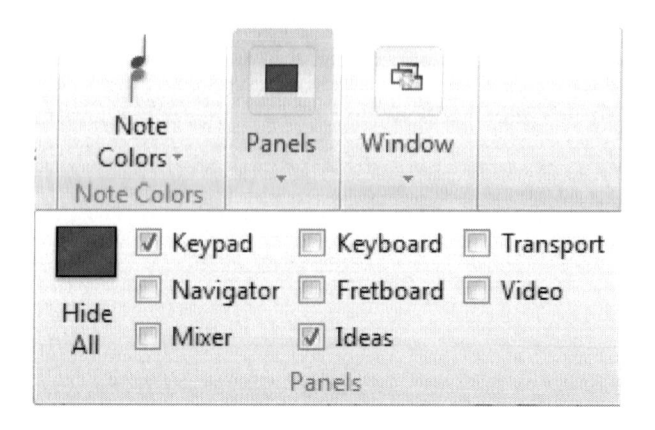

28

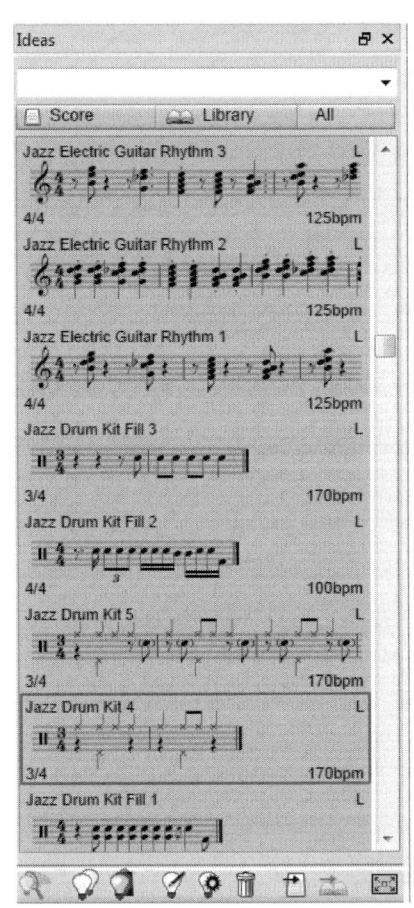

You will now see the ideas panel at the left-hand side of the screen, as seen to the left. By default it will show all the ideas it has, but it's quick and easy to find relevant ideas - click in the top white area and type the instrument you are looking for, and in the case of drums add the time signature - `drums 4/4` - and the relevant suggestions will appear.

Once you have found one you want to try, right-click on it, and pick `Copy to Clipboard`. You can then click in the place on the score you want to put the idea in, and paste it by right-clicking and picking `Paste` or hitting **CTRL+V**

The ideas panel can be extremely useful - it contains musical snippets for a wide range of instruments and situations, and can really help when you're in a rut or short of an idea. Note that if you take an idea from the bank which is in a given key, it will be transposed to suit the key of the piece where you paste it in place.

Spacing and Layout

Once you have used Sibelius for a while, you may have noticed that it controls a great deal about the layout; it has a large number of complex inter-related rules which govern the way that objects appear on the screen. However, it doesn't always get things right.

Firstly, you will often want to change the space between staves, particularly if they have text above or below them, or dynamic markings, etc. To move a staff, click the first bar so it is selected, and then move it up or down; the score will automatically be re-spaced. If you want to make this change throughout the entire score, then triple-click the bar first, and all staves will reflect the new spacing.

Next, you may want (or need) to re-space particular bars, for similar reasons to those above. To do this, click and drag on the barline that you want to move, and then you will see the rest of the score re-space to suit the new spacing. The same can also be done with individual notes. With such actions, the various rules that Sibelius employs can often take effect, and the results that you get may not always be what you desired, but typically Sibelius will respond in the most logical manner.

If you want to alter the order of instruments, go to the Home tab and click Add or Remove in the Instruments section (or press **I**). You can select the instrument you want to move in the right-hand tab, and then use the Move Up / Down buttons to get the instruments in the order you want.

Creating a score and parts from scratch

As an example of the techniques we've seen already, we will now create a score and parts using Sibelius. We'll take as an example a simple arrangement of "The Star Spangled Banner", as it contains a few characteristics that are useful to know. The score of the melody is at the back of the book, and can be downloaded as a PDF from www.musictechtuition.com

Firstly, we'll create a new score **CTRL+N**, and pick the preset with the treble staff from the `No Category` section at the top of the new score window. The window will change to look like the next one:

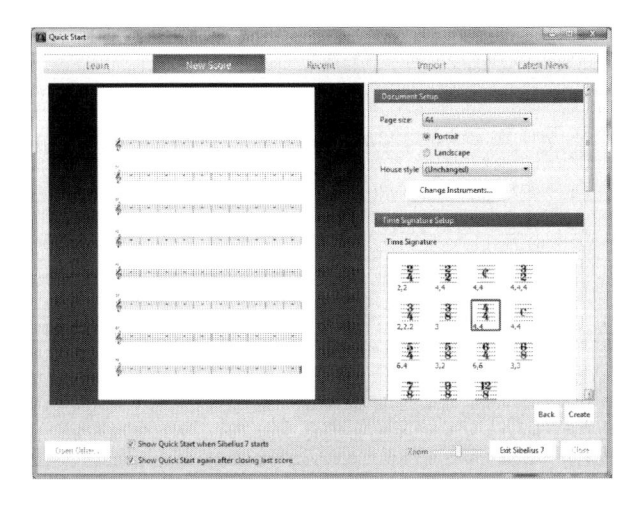

There are some options that we need to set - we can do these later on but it's quicker and easier to do them here. The first is to set the time signature - set it to 3 4, but scroll down and tick `Pick-up (Upbeat) Bar` and set it to a crotchet - our piece starts with a bar that is only a beat long:

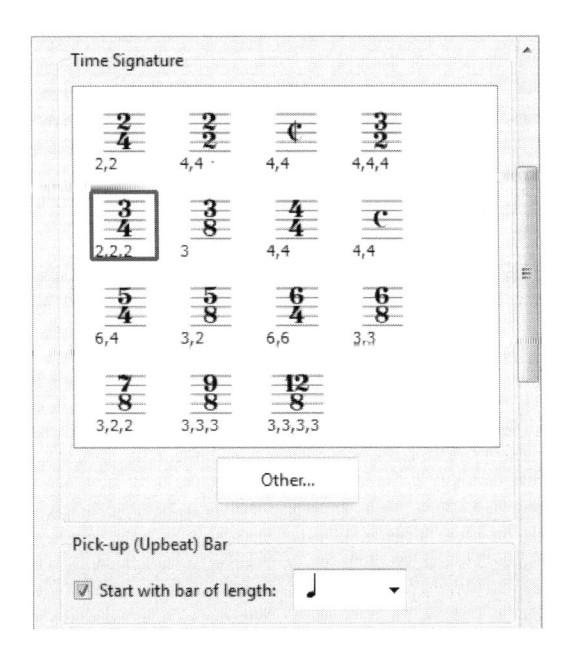

Scroll down further and the Key Signature setup area can be seen. From the drop-down menu, pick `Major flat keys` and from there pick B♭ Major.

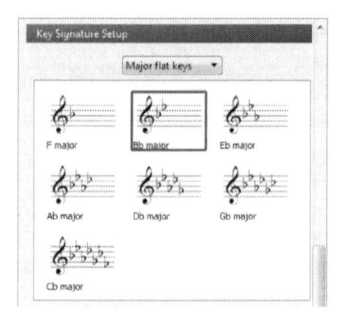

Now, click `Create` and the score will appear, with the first line looking like this:

The melody starts with an eighth-note triplet figure, so select eighth-notes (**F7** to get to note mode if you're not already there and then **3** on the numeric keypad), and then enter the first note; the melody starts with a B♭, so press **B** to enter it.

As we've already seen with triplets we then need to press **CTRL+3** to create the triplet.

Press **Num 0** for a rest, and then **G** for the final note.

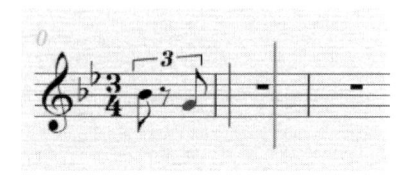

You can then use the cursor keys to go back to the initial note and change its length to the correct quarter-note (crotchet) value.

Move to the next bar, select crotchets and enter the next three notes (E, G, B♭).

The next note is a minim E, so select minim (**NUM 5**), and hit **E** on the keyboard.

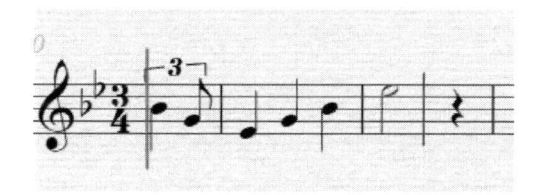

The next phrase is rhythmically identical, and can be entered in the same way as the previous phrase - start out with a quaver for the third beat of bar 2:

...and then change it to a triplet...

...and once you've entered the last note...

...turn the first one into a crotchet.

The next bar is straighforward - E, G, A, but there is a leap downwards in the melody, so entering the G on the computer keyboard puts the note in the wrong octave.

This is easily fixed by using **CTRL + ↓** to move it to the correct octave.

The rest of the melody can be added in a similar way - there is only one new feature, and that is a tie in bar 5. Enter the notes in the normal way:

And go back to select the first note in the bar (as seen above) - do this using the cursor keys. Then hit **Num Enter** and the notes will be tied.

Repeating a section

Enter the notes up to the second beat of bar 8, as seen here:

[musical notation]

Once you have this, it's time to repeat the melody again. To do this, we need to select the whole melody (including the upbeat), but **without** the rest at the end, so the upbeat will fill that gap. This is done by selecting the first note head, and then selecting the last one while holding down **SHIFT**. Your screen should then look like this:

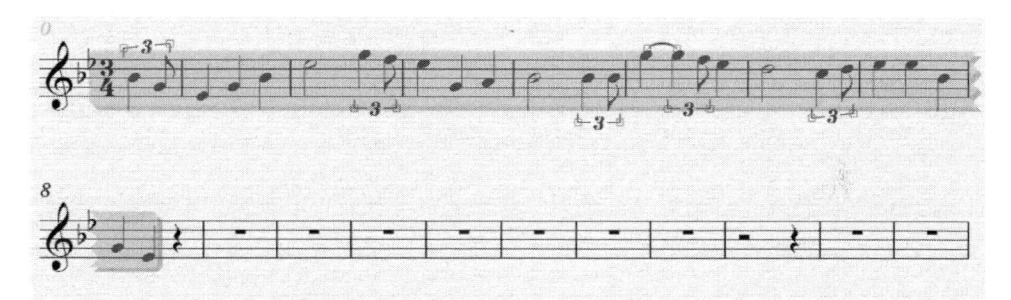

[musical notation]

To repeat the selected music, just press the **R** key, and you'll end up with the melody repeated straight after the highlighted section:

[musical notation]

To make sure that all is present and correct, select the first note, and press the 'Play' icon on the `Play` section of the ribbon (or hit **SPACE**). You should hear the melody twice through.

Now it's time to enter the second part of the melody, which is done in a similar manner, and will also involve entering a new key signature - E♭, which adds an extra A♭. To make it occur part way through a bar, hit **K** on the keyboard, pick E♭ from the menu and then place it on the third beat of bar 16.

The rhythm throughout these bars is similar, so you should find that it becomes a bit simpler to enter this section of the melody.

For the final part, the feel is changed to eighth notes, rather than triplets, and there is also an A Natural in bar 23. This can be entered from the numeric keypad either when the note is entered (press **7** before hitting **A**), or edited after the event. There are several more ties to enter, but with some work you should end up with the melody looking as shown below.

Check that all is correct by having Sibelius play the melody back to you.

Now that we have the basic melody, we'll start to create an arrangement around it; obviously the choice of instruments would be down to you to decide, but in this case we'll make it for the rather unlikely combination of trumpet, piano, guitar and violin.

Firstly, we'll create a new Instrument, in this case a Trumpet in B♭ - to do this go to the Instruments dialog box (I), and you can locate it from there. If you're not sure what section an instrument belongs in, use the `Find` section at the top to enter some of its name, and click on the one you want from the list that appears.

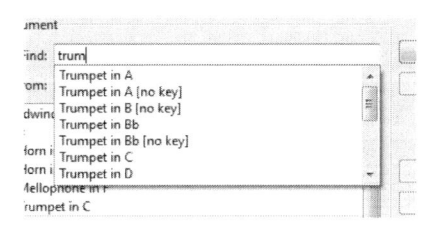

Next we want to copy the whole melody to that Instrument as it will be playing the melody for us. We do this by triple-clicking on the melody part (so that everything is selected), and then Copy (**CTRL+C**) it, and then click on the Trumpet's first bar and Paste (**CTRL+V**). You now have the melody duplicated on the Trumpet part, as shown in part below.

You may notice that the trumpet is currently at Concert pitch; this is because Sibelius is set to show Instruments at concert pitch when part of a score, but when it's an individual part (which we will cover later on), then the part is transposed to the correct pitch.

Playing back the two lines together will have a unison performance, with trumpet and piano playing together. We'll leave the trumpet as it is, and now create a Piano Instrument - again, this is done in the Instruments dialog box (**I**) and adding `Piano`, found under `Keyboards`. As with the trumpet, copy the melody to the right-hand part:

For the left-hand part, we'll use the original part as a rhythmic basis, but create a counter-melody. To do this, the first thing is to paste the melody into the left-hand part.

Once it has been pasted it will be too high, and have lots of leger lines, so we want to move the whole thing down to an appropriate pitch, which we can do using **CTRL + ↓** twice to move the whole melody down two octaves:

Now we can use this as the basis to change the notes that are present, to make a counter-melody. When retaining the rhythm like this, it's easy to just move through one note at a time to alter the pitches, either using the cursor keys or the PC or MIDI keyboard. We'll leave the choice of notes to your artistic interpretation. Remember that it's easy to replace notes, change their duration, and of course that repetition is a case of selecting the passage to be repeated, and pressing **R**.

The same procedure can be used for the violin part. Once it has been entered, add appropriate bowing marks to it, using the techniques outlined above.

Finishing touches

Along with the dynamic markings,etc that we've already seen, we can also add text to the score, with the title and composer being the most common. To do so right-click and select `Text` from the menu, and a wide range of options appears. Choose `Title` and enter the title of the piece at the top of the first page. Then add the composer too, in the same way from the right-click menu. You may notice that there are a wide range of text styles available, and each has specific characteristics which control not only its appearance, but how it is transferred to parts when they are created, as we'll see shortly. Note that once text has been created, it's possible to alter the font, size, and characteristics from the `Text` tab of the ribbon.

The Mixer

When playing back your composition, you may not be happy with the balance of instruments. If you want to alter this, press **M** to summon the mixer, as shown below.

Here is the first view of the mixer. If you play your piece back, you will see activity in the meters next to each track. There are other views of the mixer available, and these can be viewed by clicking the Mixer Height button, on the left of the mixer window:

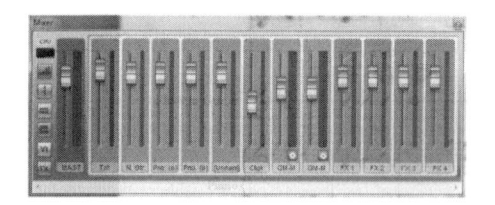

Here is the first view of the mixer, with only the faders for the channel levels in view. This will suffice for many situations.

The next view adds Mute (useful for silencing a track that you don't want to hear) and Solo buttons, as well as a pan control at the top, allowing placement in the stereo field for each track.

The third view adds controls relevant to the synthesizers that a track is being played on, with access to MIDI channel (top), synthesizer (middle) and sound (bottom) menus. This will not be needed often, but is useful for selection of a specific sound or synthesizer.

The final view adds sliders for the amount of reverb and chorus present on each track. Not all synthesizers provide these effects, but if they do then you will hear the effect here.

Mixer channel types

There are a number of different types of tracks present in the mixer, which we will now look at.

At the left there is the master output - here's it's possible to control the overall volume of the piece, which can be useful when wanting to produce a mixdown with an appropriate output level.

The next group of tracks (in blue) contains the instruments present in the score, with each track representing an instrument.

The third group of tracks (in green) contains the virtual instruments that Sibelius uses to convert the notes of the piece into sound. Each one has four effects sends which can be used to send some of that instrument's sound to one of the four effects channels that are in the next group.

The last group - effects channels - can be used to add specific audio effects to a composition, once they have been set up.

To place an effect in the track, go to `Play > Setup` and click the arrow in the bottom right to bring up the Playback Devices dialogue box. Click the `Effects` tab, and the Effects bus effects can be picked from the drop-down menus here - the effects you have will depend on what is installed on your system - and then click `Close`, and click `Yes` when asked if you want to save the changes made to the playback configuration. You will now see the effect you chose in the FX channels, and if you use the send controls from the virtual instrument tracks, you will be able to hear the effect applied to that audio.

Using the method above, it's also possible to add up to four effects to the master output, but bear in mind they will alter the sound of the entire piece so you need to choose carefully.

Creating Parts

So far, we have been working on the score, and we can use the techniques covered above to create reasonably complex scores. However, once this is done Sibelius can also create individual parts for the performers of the piece.

Go to the parts section of the ribbon, and pick `New Part`. A new window appears where it's possible to select the instruments that will be present in the part:

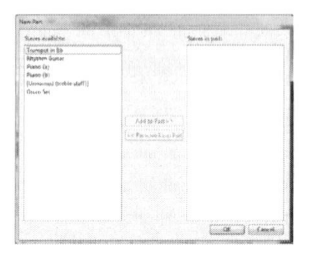

Once you have chosen the Instrument(s) to be in the part, click OK and the part will be created:

There are a few things to note - firstly, if the instrument is a transposing one, then that transposition will be applied. In this example, the instrument is a trumped in B♭, and because the original score is in B♭, the part is in C.

Secondly, the part is not "fixed" - if you make an edit in the score, it will be reflected in the part and vice-versa.

Third, Sibelius will default to using multi-rests for parts, so if there is a long passage where a performer has nothing to play, this will be represented by a bar rest symbol with the number of bars of rest written above:

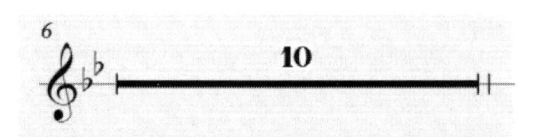

Plug-Ins

One of Sibelius' handy features is the ability to use plug-ins. These are small pieces of code which can automate certain tasks or perform certain other actions. They can be accessed from a number of the tabs of the ribbon, and the plugins available depend on which ribbon you have selected. We will look at some of the possibilities.

Brass Fingerings

In our Trumpet part, we may want to add fingerings, and under `Text > Plugins` there is a plug-in (under `Text`) which can add brass fingering; select all the music in the part, and then select the plug-in, and the correct instrument. The plug-in then works and adds the appropriate fingering:

Adding Harmony

As well as changing notation, Sibelius can help you create music. It can add parts based on ones you already have, such as the useful `Note Input > Plugins > Add Simple Harmony` plugin, which creates simple chords based on the melody you have chosen. Here is the part that it creates when selecting the Star Spangled Banner melody and using the plugin with the default settings:

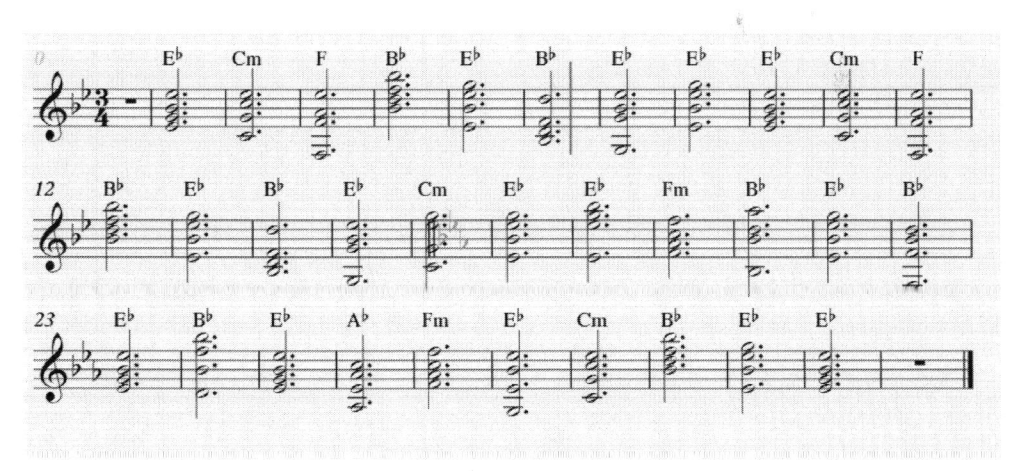

Learning what plugins are available and how they can be used is an important part of making progress with Sibelius - spend some time learning what is available and experimenting with them as often they will save you enormous amounts of time, or provide possibilities which you had not thought of.

Note Names

If you want to add note names to the heads of the notes to make a part easier to read for some players, it would be possible to do this for each note, but the plugin will automate the process. To do this, select the entire part (by triple-clicking on a bar), and then picking Home > Plugins > Add Note Names to Noteheads. Once you have decided whether to do it to the selected passage or the whole score, the plugin runs, and here is the result:

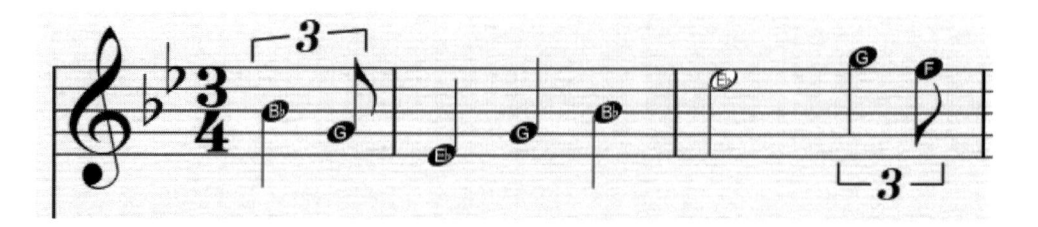

Transformations

In a similar manner to the plugins we have just seen, Sibelius can perform musical transformations on your existing material, speeding up the process of composition and/or arrangement greatly. The following actions are all found under the Note Input tab of the ribbon. They will all be applied to the following phrase:

Double

The length of each note is doubled, and the phrase is copied into a new score (you can then copy it back to wherever you like in your original).

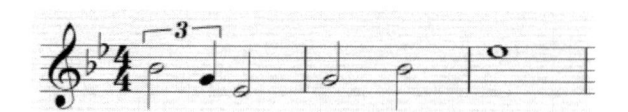

Halve

The length of each note is halved, and the phrase is copied into a new score (you can then copy it back to wherever you like in your original).

Retrograde

The original phrase is reversed, replacing the original:

Invert

A dialogue box appears, where you can pick the note around which the phrase is to be inverted (often this will be the first note of the phrase), and whether to invert the phrase diatonically (usually the best choice) or chromatically.

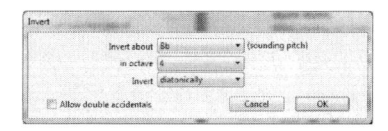

Once performed, the result is this:

Augment Intervals

This increases the intervals by the selected amount in the melody, increasing the space between each note, 'widening' the melody's intervals.

Diminish Intervals

This decreases the intervals by the selected amount in the melody, decreasing the space between each note, 'narrowing' the melody's intervals.

Randomize Pitches

The pitches of the original phrase are replaced by random ones:

Rotate Pitches

As the name suggests, this rotates the pitches, so that the last one becomes the first, and all the others move one position later in the phrase:

Each of these transformations will obviously depend on the original material that you are transforming, but using them can greatly speed up any of these processes, as well as allow you to experiment with new ideas for very little effort.

Arranging

Sibelius has an "arrange" feature which allows the creation of arrangements from a simple piece of source material. However, it is important to remember that it is really an intelligent copy and paste function – it alters your source material using some simple rules which control which instruments it will paste onto , and which passage of music will be pasted to where, as well as doubling other parts by a specific interval.

There is a wide range of Arrange styles provided with Sibelius, and it is possible to alter them as well, giving a huge range of possibilities.

Creating your source material

The first thing to remember is that the Arrange function needs source material to work with – it doesn't actually generate anything, just takes what you put into it and works with that. For best results, you will want at least three parts created; for good quick results you should find that three parts works well – melody, chords and a bassline – Sibelius will use distribute these amongst the destination parts depending on rules which will alter depending on each arrangement style, and picks them depending on which is the highest, lowest, busiest or fastest. Here is the source material we will be working with throughout this handout – the first 8 bars of the Star Spangled Banner, with the melody on one staff, and a simple piano accompaniment consisting of root-position triads and a bass part of the root notes of these chords.

Creating the Arrangement

The first step in the new arrangement is to create the Instruments that you want the piece arranged onto – in this first example we will be using a typical 4-part choir arrangement, with Soprano, Alto, Tenor and Bass. These are created using the "Instruments" dialog, accessed by pressing **I**

Once these have been created, select the music to be arranged. In this case it is the entire piece, on all three of the original staves. To do this, click once at the beginning on the top instrument (in this case inside bar 1 on the melody), and then move to the end, hold down **SHIFT** and click in the last bar of the bottom Instrument (in this case, inside bar 8 of the left-hand piano part). The screen will look something like the one shown below.

Once you have selected the material you wish to arrange, copy it, either using the menu (Home > Copy) or **CTRL+C**.

Next, select the instruments and bars you wish Sibelius to arrange onto – this is done in a similar manner to the selection of the source material. Note that you don't *have* to use the same bars, but typically you will do so. Once you have selected all the bars of the four voices we wish to arrange onto, the screen should look something like the one to the next page.

Now it's time to go to the Arrange section, which is found under `Note input > Arrange` or **CTRL+SHIFT+V**. You will see a new dialog box like the one seen here:

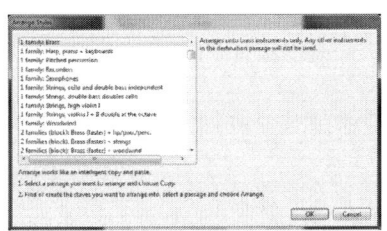

Here you can scroll through the preset Arrange styles which are provided with Sibelius, and see a short description of what each one does. In this case we will look at some of the different "Choir" arrangements, which you can scroll to, or just hit **C** on the keyboard to jump there.

For the first arrangement, we will use `Choir: Standard`, which will produce a standard choir arrangement, with the information we have input split between the staves. Here we see the result of this on the first 5 bars – the melody has been moved to the Soprano part, while the chords have been split beween the Alto and Tenor parts. The bass line has been moved to the bass part.

As you can see, the Arrange function has intelligently moved the source musical material to the appropriate staves, saving what would otherwise be a quite tedious and multi-stage job. It hasn't created anything new from the original source.

There are, however, a number of different arrangement functions for the Choir provided by Sibelius. Next, we'll use `Choir: Tune in A,` which is largely similar to the previous function, but moves the tune to the Alto part.

As you can see, the Tenor and Bass parts are the same as the previous example, but the Soprano and Alto parts are swapped over.

There are other variations on this arrangement, with the melody being in the Tenor or Bass parts, and Sibelius will transpose the melody to suit the Instrument range if possible; note that in this example there are a couple of notes which are out of range and are marked accordingly – you would need to tidy this up manually via whatever means you found appropriate, another demonstration that the Arrange feature is not a total substitute for human skills!

Next we will try `T doubling S down 8ve, B doubling A down 8ve` – in this case the material is arranged according to new rules, and the Bass and Tenor parts are octave-down doubles of the Alto and Soprano parts respectively.

This may not be entirely satisfactory and to rectify this a mixture of arrangement styles may be needed – see later for this.

Arranging into a new Score

So far the arranging has been done within an existing score, with the Instruments being added to that score and then selected and arranged into – this is sometimes how you will work, adding new instruments to an existing score, and it also served to demonstrate how the source material was distributed by the arrange function. It is important to remember that you do not have to work like this – it can be quite long-winded adding instruments to an existing score, and you may already have saved a manuscript of your own allowing you to create a new score with the settings you wish very quickly. In this case we will take the Star Spangled Banner and use the arrange function to create a full orchestral score.

Firstly, we select the source material as we did in the first example, selecting the first and last bars of the instruments we wish to use, and copying them (`File > Copy` or **CTRL+C**).

Now create a new Score (`File > New...`) and pick the manuscript you wish to use – in this case `Orchestra, Modern` and made the relevant changes for this piece (in 3/4 time with a one beat anacrusis, and in B♭ Major), and the result is an empty score for a full orchestra – clearly this would have taken some time to create manually, as it contains 34 instruments!

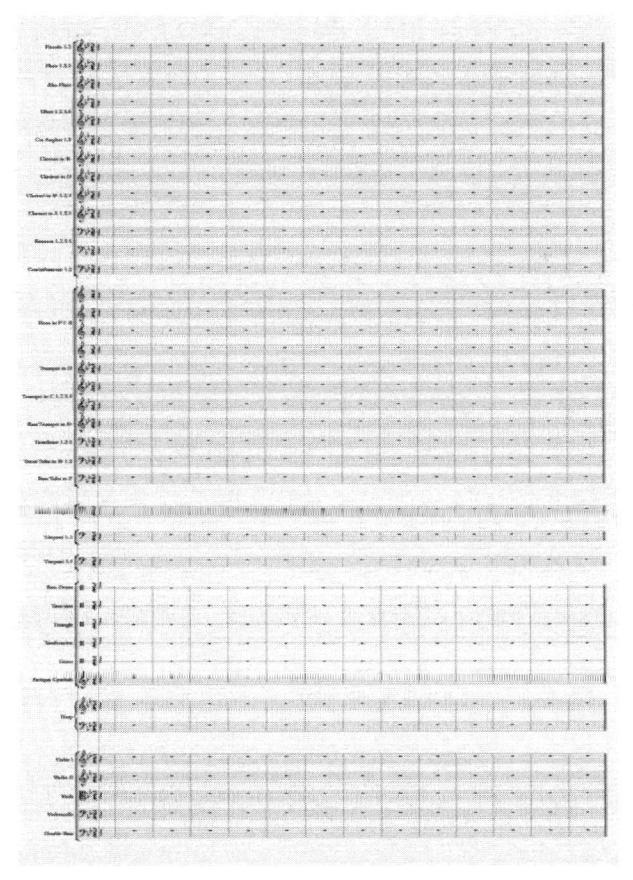

Next, as before, select the instruments and bar ranges to be used – in this case, 9 bars across all instruments as the arrange style will only use the instruments that it is set to.

Finally, select `Note Input > Arrange` and pick the relevant style – in this example, `Orchestra, Film: Main Theme` has been selected, which has created the following arrangement – we can see that while some sections of the orchestra have been catered for, there are others which are currently silent.

This might not be what you are after, so we will now add to this by using different arrange styles on some of the 'missing' sections – it is possible to use different arrange styles (for a different arrangement, or simply to fill in instruments which were not catered for by the original style that you used) – firstly we will arrange for the Clarinets.

To do this, we need to select the Clarinets only on our score, as seen below

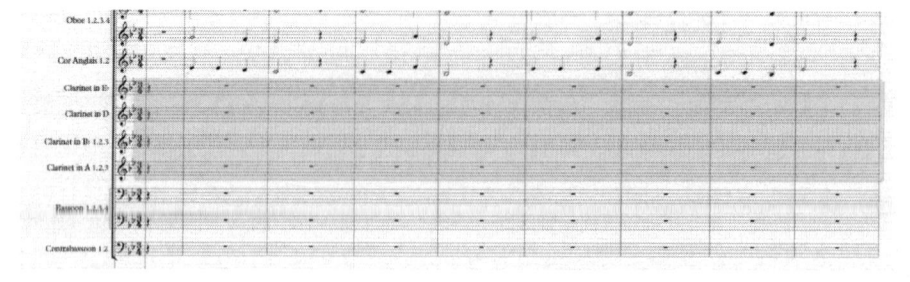

Next, we will pick a new arrange style, in this case `1 Family: Woodwind` which will produce the following arrangement.

In the same manner, the Timpani can be arranged using the `1 Family: Pitched Percussion` arrange style:

One area where there isn't a pre-set Arrange style is for unpitched percussion. However, as a two-step process the arrangement can be tried, to preserve the rhythm of the source material while fixing the pitches correctly. In this example, we will use the `Explode` arrange style to place the notes on the unpitched percussion instruments, as shown:

This doesn't give a satisfactory result – for instance, for the triangle to play correctly, it needs to be a specific pitch, and currently it could be any note of an entire drum kit.

Firstly, select the notes of the Triangle part alone (as shown above). The next step is to fix the pitches of the notes to the appropriate ones. This is done with one of Sibelius' Plug-Ins, under `Note Input > Plug-Ins > Notes and Rests > Make Pitches Constant`.

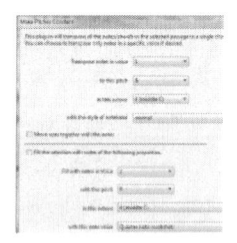

Above we can see the Plug-in's settings, and in this case we will be transposing the notes in voice 1 (the default, shown in blue when selected) to the pitch B4 – this is the correct note for the triangle. Click OK and the result should be as shown on the next page.

As we can see, the triangle is now fixed to the correct pitch, and plays correctly. Some Instruments will play correctly having been fixed to a B (the centre line on the staff), while others will not. However, as you have them all selected, it is simply a case of using the ↑ and ↓ arrows on the keyboard to move the entire part to the desired pitch.

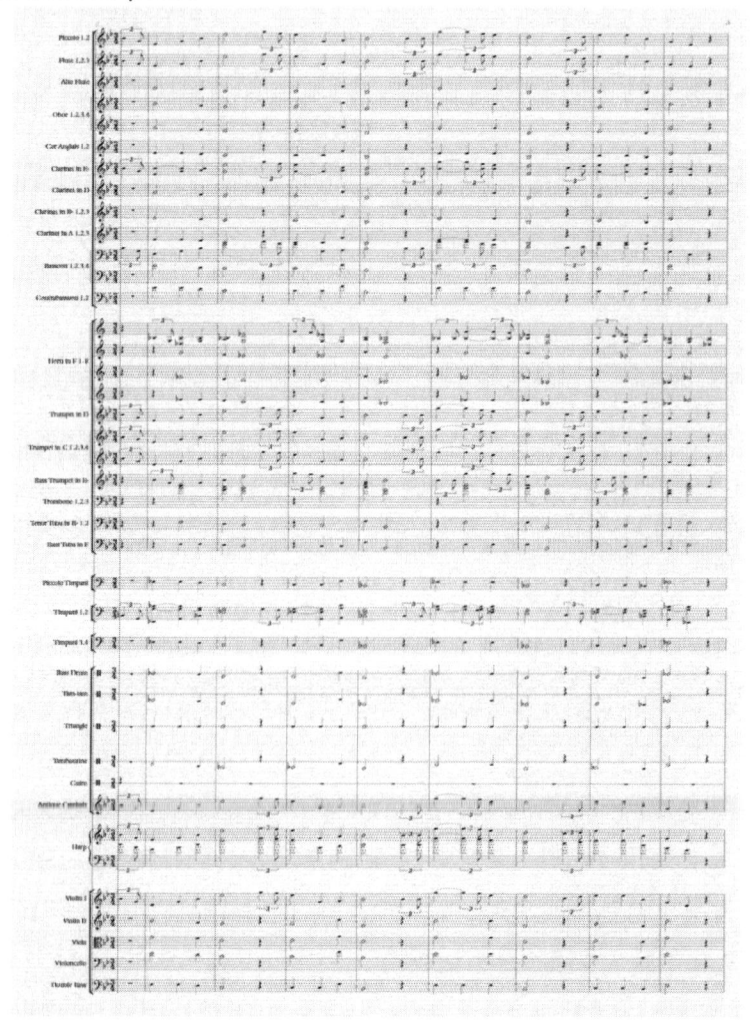

On the previous page is the final version of the arrangement for the orchestra – at present this has only been created using the Arrange function, without any manual editing of notes, which would usually be the next step – this arrangement was achieved in very little time, and when using this function you can usually be confident that there have not been errors in transposition of parts when copying from one instrument to another.

Summary

The Arrange function in Sibelius is a very useful tool for creating arrangements of a source piece of music, but it can only work with the information you give it and distribute that information using some simple (but powerful) rules. Each arrangement style can produce a different result based on these rules, and is capable of creating large, complex arrangements of material with very little time spent when compared with arranging the same material manually. It is not a complete solution, and the parts generated will then need to be edited to be musically suitable, but it saves a great deal of time.

Score Styles

When creating our initial score, we just chose a basic empty A4 style. However, there are a great number of styles that Sibelius has, including a wide range of preset band line-ups, and also using the 'Inkpen' style, which lends a handwritten style to the music, as shown with the two examples below (from the Jazz section of the new score).

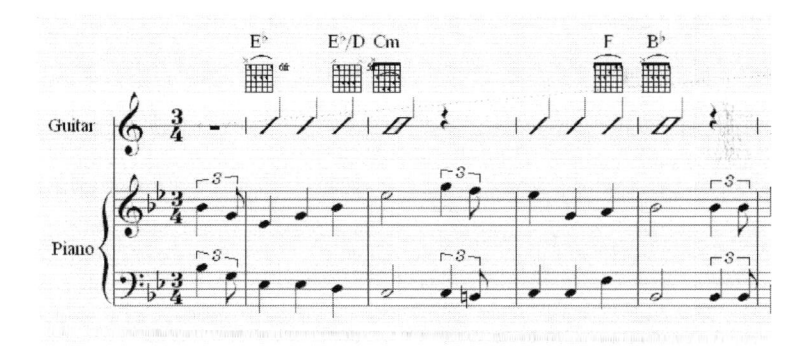

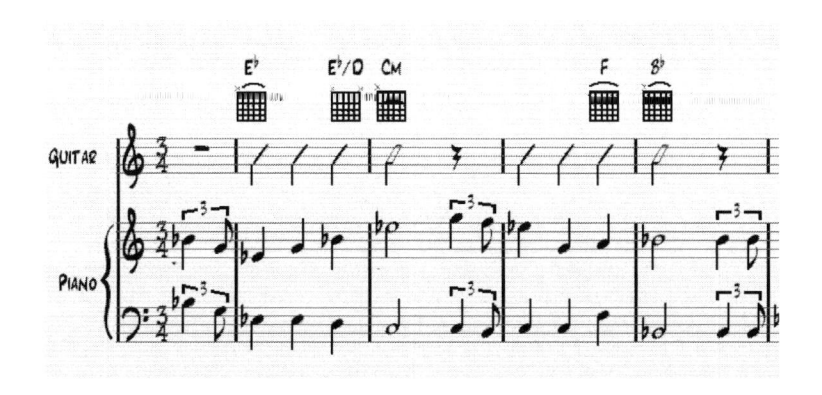

Exporting your work

When you have finished your score, you may well want to export it. While printing is often an option (`File > Print` or **CTRL+P**), there are times when you will want to export the score in different formats:

PDF

A PDF is useful when wanting to transfer a score over the Internet. To create one, go to `File > Export` and pick `PDF`. You can then choose what you want to export (score, parts or combination thereof), where to place it and what it will be called - usually the default filename will suffice as it uses the score and part name. You will need to scroll down to the Export button and click it to export your PDF.

MIDI

The notes that you have entered can be exported as a MIDI file which can then be imported on a sequencing package such as Cubase or Logic, or for quick and easy transfer over the Internet for others to play or work on. Once more, go to `File > Export and` pick `MIDI`, and usually the default options will be sufficient to create a MIDI file usable by others. Clicking `Export` will summon a file selector box where you can pick where to save the MIDI file and what to call it.

Audio

An audio file of your piece can often be useful for a number of reasons, and exporting one from Sibelius is quick and easy to do. Go to File > Export and pick Audio, and then you can select options - usually the Playback configuration and Playback line will be fine with the defaults, and then you can pick a name and location for your audio file. The bit depth and sample rate should normally be left at 16 bit and 44.1kHz for most purposes. Clicking Export will generate a WAV file, which will be quite large in size (usually too large to email or for people to download), so you may want to use a program such as Format Factory to convert your WAV file to an MP3 or other compressed audio format.

Keyboard Shortcuts

The following is a list of useful keyboard shortcuts when using Sibelius. There are many others, but knowing these is a good start, and using the keyboard instead of the mouse is the key to becoming quick, efficient and accurate when entering music in Sibelius.

File related

New	CTRL+N
Open	CTRL+O
Close	CTRL+W
Save	CTRL+S

Creating Notes

Note input mode	N
Note lengths	NUM 1 - NUM 6
Natural / Sharp / Flat	NUM 7 - NUM 9
Dotted note	NUM .
Note Pitch	A-G on keyboard
Rest	NUM 0
Add an interval above	1-9
Add an interval below	SHIFT 1 - SHIFT 9
Add a pitch above	SHIFT A - SHIFT G

Adding elements

Expression text	CTRL+E
f,m,p in expression	CTRL+F, CTRL+M, CTRL+P
Key signature	K
Time signature	SHIFT+T
Clef	Q
Add Instruments	I
Chord Symbol	CTRL+K
Slur	S
Crescendo	H
Diminuendo	SHIFT+H
Triplet	CTRL+3
Tempo	CTRL+ALT+T

The Star Spangled Banner

Here is the lead sheet for the Star Spangled Banner, used as an example in the book.

Printed in Great Britain
by Amazon.co.uk, Ltd.,
Marston Gate.